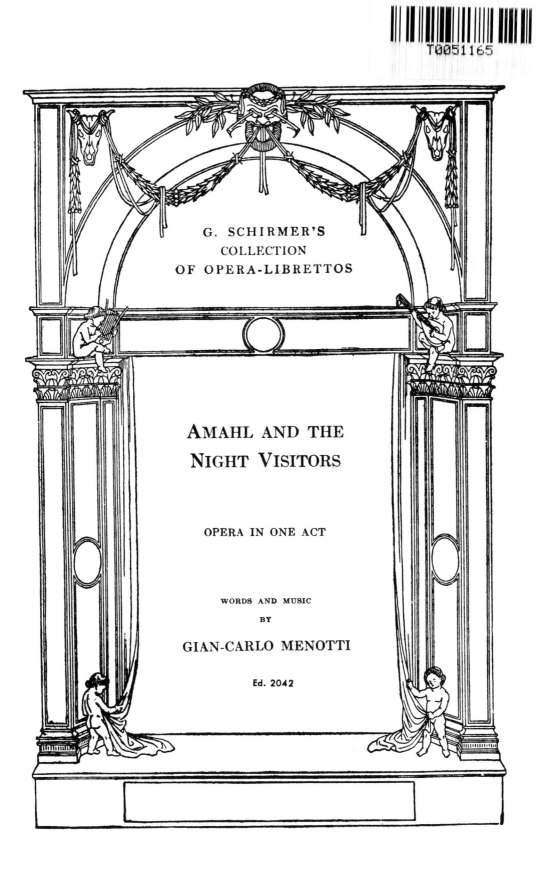

G. SCHIRMER'S
COLLECTION
OF OPERA-LIBRETTOS

AMAHL AND THE NIGHT VISITORS

OPERA IN ONE ACT

WORDS AND MUSIC
BY

GIAN-CARLO MENOTTI

Ed. 2042

G. SCHIRMER, Inc.

42824c

Cast of Characters

AMAHL (a crippled boy of about 12)

HIS MOTHER

KASPAR (slightly deaf) }

MELCHIOR } *The Three Kings*

BALTHAZAR }

THE PAGE

CHORUS OF SHEPHERDS AND VILLAGERS

DANCERS

AMAHL AND THE NIGHT VISITORS

(The curtain rises. It is night. The crystal-clear winter sky is dotted with stars, the Eastern Star flaming amongst them. Outside the cottage, not far from its door, Amahl, wrapped in an oversized cloak, sits on a stone, playing his shepherd's pipe. His crudely-made crutch lies on the ground beside him. Within, the Mother works at household chores. The room is lighted only by the dying fire and the low flame of a tiny oil lamp.)

THE MOTHER
(She pauses in her work to listen to the piping, then calls.)
Amahl! Amahl!

AMAHL
Oh!

THE MOTHER
Time to go to bed!

AMAHL
Coming!
(Amahl does not stir. After a moment he begins to play again.)

THE MOTHER
Amahl!

AMAHL
Coming!
(With a shrug of his shoulders, Amahl continues to play. Impatiently, the Mother goes to the window, opens it sharply, and leans out.)

THE MOTHER
How long must I shout to make you obey?

AMAHL
I'm sorry, Mother.

THE MOTHER
Hurry in! It's time to go to bed.

AMAHL
But Mother, let me stay a little longer!

THE MOTHER
The wind is cold.

AMAHL
But my cloak is warm,
let me stay a little longer!

THE MOTHER
The night is dark.

AMAHL
But the sky is light,
let me stay a little longer!

THE MOTHER
The time is late.

AMAHL
But the moon hasn't risen yet,
let me stay a little . . .

THE MOTHER
(clapping her hands)
There won't be any moon tonight.
But there will be a weeping child very soon,
if he doesn't hurry up and obey his mother.
(The Mother closes the window with a sharp little bang.)

AMAHL
Oh, very well.
(Reluctantly, Amahl rises, takes up his crutch, and hobbles
into the house. On the pegs to one side of the door he hangs
his heavy cloak and shepherd's cap. His pipe he places
carefully in the corner. The Mother kneels at the fireplace,

trying to coax a flame from the few remaining twigs. Amahl returns to the open door and leans against it, looking up to the sky.)

THE MOTHER
What was keeping you outside?

AMAHL
Oh, Mother, you should go out and see!
There's never been such a sky!
Damp clouds have shined it
and soft winds have swept it
as if to make it ready for a King's ball.
All its lanterns are lit,
all its torches are burning,
and its dark floor
is shining like crystal.
Hanging over our roof
there is a star as large as a window,
and the star has a tail,
and it moves across the sky
like a chariot on fire.

THE MOTHER
(wearily)
Oh! Amahl, when will you stop telling lies?
All day long you wander about in a dream.
Here we are with nothing to eat,
not a stick of wood on the fire,
not a drop of oil in the jug,
and all you do is to worry your mother
with fairy tales.
Oh! Amahl, have you forgotten your promise
never, never to lie to your mother again?

AMAHL
Mother darling, I'm not lying.
Please, do believe me.

(He tugs at her skirt.)
Come outside and let me show you.
See for yourself . . . See for yourself . . .

THE MOTHER
(She brushes his hand aside.)
Stop bothering me! Why should I believe you?
You come with a new one every day!
First it was a leopard with a woman's head.
Then it was a tree branch that shrieked and bled.
Then it was a fish as big as a boat,
with whiskers like a cat and wings like a bat
and horns like a goat.
And now it is a star as large as a window . . .
or was it a carriage . . .
And if that weren't enough,
the star has a tail and the tail is of fire!

AMAHL
But there is a star and it has a tail this long.
*(Amahl measures the air as wide as his arms can reach. At
her frown, he reduces the size by half.)*
Well, maybe only . . . this long. But it's there!

THE MOTHER
Amahl!

AMAHL
Cross my heart and hope to die.

THE MOTHER
(clasping Amahl in her arms)
Poor Amahl!
Hunger has gone to your head.
Dear God, what is a poor widow to do,
when her cupboards and pockets are empty
and everything sold?

(She moves disconsolately to the fireplace.)

Unless we go begging
how shall we live through tomorrow?
My little son, a beggar!

(She sinks, weeping, onto a little stool. Amahl goes to her and embraces her tenderly, stroking her hair.)

AMAHL

Don't cry, Mother dear,
don't worry for me.
If we must go begging,
a good beggar I'll be.
I know sweet tunes to set people dancing.
We'll walk and walk from village to town,
you dressed as a gypsy and I as a clown.
At noon we shall eat roast goose and sweet
    almonds,
at night we shall sleep with the sheep and the
    stars.
I'll play my pipes, you'll sing and you'll shout.
The windows will open and people lean out.
The King will ride by and hear your loud voice
and throw us some gold to stop all the noise.
At noon we shall eat roast goose and sweet
    almonds,
at night we shall sleep with the sheep and the
    stars.

THE MOTHER

My dreamer, good night!
You're wasting the light.
Kiss me good night.

AMAHL

Good night.

(The Mother rises and bends to receive the good-night kiss. Amahl goes to his pallet of straw at one side of the fireplace. The Mother secures the door, takes Amahl's cloak and spreads it over him, touches his head tenderly, then, having snuffed out the tiny oil lamp, she lies down on the bench. The lights die from the room except for a faint glow in the fireplace and the radiance of the sky through the window.)

(In the distance among the hills, we see a tiny winking light from a lantern, then the small figures of the Three Kings and the Page, wending their way along the mountain road. Amahl raises himself on one elbow and listens with astonishment to the distant singing. The figures disappear at a turn in the road. Amahl throws back his cloak and, leaning on his crutch, hobbles over to the window. At the left, on the road, appear the Three Kings: first Melchior, bearing the coffer of gold, then Balthazar, bearing the chalice of myrrh, and finally Kaspar, bearing the urn of incense. All are preceded by the Page, who walks heavily, bent beneath the load of many bundles, among them a rich Oriental rug, a caged parrot, and an elaborate jeweled box. In one hand the Page carries a heavy lantern to light the way.)

KASPAR, MELCHIOR, BALTHAZAR

From far away we come and farther we must go.
How far, how far, my crystal star?
The shepherd dreams inside the fold.
Cold are the sands by the silent sea.
Frozen the incense in our frozen hands,
heavy the gold.
How far, how far, my crystal star?
By silence-sunken lakes the antelope leaps.
In paper-painted oasis the drunken gypsy weeps.
The hungry lion wanders, the cobra sleeps.
How far, how far, my crystal star?

(As the travelers approach the door of the cottage, the Page steps aside to let King Melchior knock upon the door.)

THE MOTHER

(*Without stirring from her bed*)
    Amahl, go and see who's knocking at the door.

AMAHL

    Yes, Mother.
(*Amahl goes to the door and opens it a crack. He quickly
closes the door and rushes to his mother.*)
    Mother, Mother, Mother, come with me.
    I want to be sure that you see what I see.

THE MOTHER

(*raising herself on her elbow*)
    What is the matter with you now?
    What is all this fuss about?
    Who is it then?

AMAHL

(*hesitatingly*)
    Mother . . . outside the door there is . . .
    there is a King with a crown.

THE MOTHER

    What shall I do with this boy,
    what shall I do?
    If you don't learn to tell the truth,
    I'll have to spank you!
(*Knocks. After a pause she sinks back on the bed.*)
    Go back and see who it is
    and ask them what they want.
(*Amahl hurries to the door, again opens it just a crack, and
stares. He closes it once more and returns to his mother.*)

AMAHL

    Mother, Mother . . . Mother, come with me.
    I want to be sure that you see what I see.

THE MOTHER
What is the matter with you now,
what is all this fuss about?

AMAHL
Mother . . . I didn't tell the truth before.

THE MOTHER
That's a good boy.

AMAHL
There is not a King outside.

THE MOTHER
I should say not!

AMAHL
There are two Kings!

THE MOTHER
What shall I do with this boy,
what shall I do?
Hurry back and see who it is,
and don't you dare make up tales!
(Amahl repeats again the action to the door and back.)

AMAHL
Mother . . . Mother . . . Mother, come with me.
If I tell you the truth,
I know you won't believe me.

THE MOTHER
Try it for a change!

AMAHL
But you won't believe me.

THE MOTHER
I'll believe you if you tell the truth.

AMAHL

Sure enough, there are not two Kings outside.

THE MOTHER

That is surprising.

AMAHL

The Kings are three,
and one of them is black.

THE MOTHER

Oh! What shall I do with this boy!
If you were stronger I'd like to whip you.

AMAHL

I knew it!

THE MOTHER

I'm going to the door myself,
and then, young man,
you'll have to reckon with me!

*(The Mother rises wearily and moves determinedly to the
door. Amahl follows, holding onto her skirt. As the door
swings open, she beholds the Three Kings. In utter amaze-
ment, she bows to them.)*

KASPAR, MELCHIOR, BALTHAZAR

Good evening!

AMAHL

(whispering)
What did I tell you?

THE MOTHER

(to Amahl)
Sh!
(to the Kings)
Noble sires!

BALTHAZAR
May we rest a while in your house
and warm ourselves by your fireplace?

THE MOTHER
I am a poor widow.
A cold fireplace and a bed of straw
are all I have to offer you.
To these you are welcome.

KASPAR
(cupping his ear)
What did she say?

BALTHAZAR
That we are welcome.

KASPAR
(excitedly)
Oh, thank you, thank you,
thank you!
(Melchior and Balthazar tap Kaspar's shoulder to restrain him.)

KASPAR, MELCHIOR, BALTHAZAR
Oh, thank you!

THE MOTHER
Come in, come in!
(Still bowing, the Mother makes way for the King to enter, pulling Amahl with her. The Page enters first, places his lantern on the stool beside the fireplace, and drops his bundles. Almost immediately, King Kaspar proceeds at a stately march to take his place on the bench, stage right. The Page hurries to hold King Kaspar's train. Once Kaspar has placed himself, Balthazar enters and proceeds to a place beside him. Melchior is the last to take his place. The Page runs back and forth to carry the trains of each. When the Three Kings

*are together, they sit as one. The Page spreads the rug before
them and sets upon it the gifts the Kings bear for the Child.
Amahl watches the procession with growing wonder and
excitement.)*

MELCHIOR

It is nice here.

THE MOTHER

I shall go and gather wood for the fire.
I've nothing in the house.

*(The Mother takes her shawl from the peg and goes to the
door.)*

MELCHIOR

We can only stay a little while.
We must not lost sight of our star.

THE MOTHER

Your star?

AMAHL

(whispering to his mother)
What did I tell you?

THE MOTHER

Sh!

MELCHIOR

We still have a long way to go.

THE MOTHER

I shall be right back . . . and Amahl
don't be a nuisance

(She goes quickly.)

AMAHL

No, Mother.

*(The moment his mother is gone, Amahl goes to Balthazar.
Kaspar goes to the corner of the fireplace where the Page
has placed the parrot and the jeweled box. During the fol-
lowing scene he feeds the parrot bits of food from his pocket.)*
Are you a real King?

BALTHAZAR

Yes.

AMAHL

Have you regal blood?

BALTHAZAR

Yes.

AMAHL

Can I see it?

BALTHAZAR

It is just like yours.

AMAHL

What's the use of having it, then?

BALTHAZAR

No use.

AMAHL

Where is your home?

BALTHAZAR

I live in a black marble palace
full of black panthers and white doves.
And you, little boy,
what do you do?

AMAHL

(sadly)

I was a shepherd, I had a flock of sheep.
But my mother sold them.
Now there are no sheep left.
I had a black goat who gave me warm sweet milk.
But she died of old age.
Now there is no goat left.
But Mother says that now
we shall both go begging from door to door.
Won't it be fun?

BALTHAZAR

It has its points.
(Amahl crosses to Kaspar, who continues to feed the parrot.)

AMAHL

Are you a real King, too?

KASPAR

Eh?
(Amahl looks wonderingly at Balthazar, who indicates that Kaspar is deaf. Amahl repeats the question, shouting.)

AMAHL

ARE YOU A REAL KING, TOO?

KASPAR

Oh, truly, truly, yes.
I am a real King . . . am I not?
(Kaspar looks questioningly at Balthazar.)

BALTHAZAR

Yes, Kaspar.

AMAHL

What is that?

KASPAR

Eh?

AMAHL

WHAT IS THAT?

KASPAR

A parrot.

AMAHL

Does it talk?

KASPAR

Eh?

AMAHL

DOES IT TALK?

KASPAR

(indicating his deaf ears)
How do I know?

AMAHL

Does it bite?

KASPAR

Eh?

AMAHL

DOES IT BITE?
(Kaspar displays a heavily bandaged finger.)

KASPAR

Yes.

AMAHL

(pointing at the jeweled box)
And what is this?
(With great excitement, Kaspar opens one drawer at a time, concealing its contents from Amahl until he lifts the jewels, the beads, and finally the licorice before the boy's amazed eyes.)

KASPAR

This is my box, this is my box.
I never travel without my box.
In the first drawer I keep my magic stones.
One carnelian against all evil and envy.
One moonstone to make you sleep.
One red coral to heal your wounds.
One lapis lazuli against quartern fever.
One small jasper to help you find water.
One small topaz to soothe your eyes.
One red **ruby to protect you from lightning.**

This is my box, this is my box.
I never travel without my box.
In the second drawer I keep all my beads.
Oh, how I love to play with beads,
all kinds of beads.
This is my box, this is my box.
I never travel without my box.
In the third drawer . . .
Oh, little boy! Oh, little boy! . . .
In the third drawer I keep . . .
licorice . . . black, sweet licorice.
Have some.

*(Amahl seizes the candy and gobbles it down as his mother
enters from the outside, bearing a few sticks.)*

THE MOTHER
Amahl, I told you not to be a nuisance!

AMAHL
But it isn't my fault!
(Going to his mother, Amahl whispers discreetly.)
They kept asking me questions.

THE MOTHER
I want you to go and call the other shepherds.
Tell them about our visitors,
and ask them to bring
whatever they have in the house,
as we have nothing to offer them.
Hurry on!

AMAHL
Yes, Mother.

*(Amahl grabs up his cloak, claps his hat on his head, and
hurries out as fast as his crutch will carry him. The Mother
crosses to the fireplace to set down the wood she has gathered.
Suddenly she sees the coffer of gold, and the rich chalices of
incense and myrrh which sit before the Kings. Irresistibly
drawn, she moves toward them.)*

THE MOTHER
Oh, these beautiful things . . .
and all that gold!

MELCHIOR
These are the gifts to the Child.

THE MOTHER
(with great excitement)
The child?
Which child?

MELCHIOR
We don't know.
But the Star will guide us to Him.

THE MOTHER
But perhaps I know him.
What does he look like?

MELCHIOR
Have you seen a Child
the color of wheat, the color of dawn?
His eyes are mild,
His hands are those of a King,
as King He was born.
Incense, myrrh, and gold
we bring to His side,
and the Eastern Star is our guide.

THE MOTHER
(as though to herself)
Yes, I know a child
the color of wheat, the color of dawn.
His eyes are mild,
his hands are those of a King,
as King he was born.

But no one will bring him incense or gold,
though sick and poor and hungry and cold.
He's my child, my son,
my darling, my own.

MELCHIOR, BALTHAZAR

Have you seen a Child
the color of earth, the color of thorn?
His eyes are sad,
His hands are those of the poor,
as poor He was born.
Incense, myrrh, and gold
we bring to His side,
and the Eastern Star is our guide.

THE MOTHER

Yes, I know a child
the color of earth, the color of thorn.
His eyes are sad,
his hands are those of the poor,
as poor he was born.
But no one will bring him incense or gold,
though sick and poor and hungry and cold.
He's my child, my son,
my darling, my own.

MELCHIOR

The Child we seek holds the seas
and the winds on His palm.

KASPAR

The Child we seek has the moon
and the stars at His feet.

BALTHAZAR

Before Him the eagle is gentle,
the lion is meek.

(Absorbed in her own thoughts, the Mother moves slowly downstage.)

THE MOTHER

The child I know
on his palm holds my heart.
The child I know
at his feet has my life.
He's my child, my son,
my darling, my own,
and his name is Amahl.

KASPAR, MELCHIOR, BALTHAZAR

Choirs of angels hover over His roof
and sing Him to sleep.
He's warmed by breath,
He's fed by Mother
who is both Virgin and Queen.
Incense, myrrh, and gold
we bring to His side,
and the Eastern Star is our guide.

(The call of the shepherds falls sharp and clear on the air, breaking the hushed silence of the room.)

SHEPHERDS

Shepherds! Shepherdesses!
Who's calling, who's calling?
Oh! Oh!

(The Mother looks instinctively to see if her room is ready to receive her neighbors, then she goes to the door and opens it wide.)

THE MOTHER

The shepherds are coming!

MELCHIOR

(He nudges the dozing Kaspar.)

Wake up, Kaspar!

(First singly, then in twos and threes, the shepherds begin to appear. They come from all directions. On the hills in the distance lantern lights pierce the darkness. Slowly they converge and move down the road toward the hut, led by a radiant Amahl.)

SHEPHERDS

Emily, Emily,
Michael, Bartholomew,
how are your children and how are your sheep?
Dorothy, Dorothy,
Peter, Evangeline,
give me your hand, come along with me,
All the children have mumps.
All the flocks are asleep.
We are going with Amahl, bringing gifts to the
    Kings.
Benjamin, Benjamin,
Lucas, Elizabeth,
how are your children and how are your sheep?
Carolyn, Carolyn,
Matthew, Veronica,
give me your hand, come along with me.

(Ragged and joyous, the shepherds approach the hut, bearing their baskets of fruit and vegetables.)

Brrr! How cold is the night!
Brrr! How icy the wind!
Hold me very, very, very tight.
Oh, how warm is your cloak!
Katherine, Katherine,
Christopher, Babila,
how are your children and how are your sheep?
Josephine, Josephine,
Angela, Jeremy,

come along with me.
Oh! look!
Oh! look!
(The shepherds crowd together in the frame of the door of the hut, struck dumb by the sight of the Kings, not daring to enter. Amahl, however, slips through the crowd to take his place beside his mother.)

THE MOTHER

Come in, come in!
What are you afraid of?
(Shy and embarrassed, everyone tries to push his neighbor in ahead of him, until all of them are crowded into one corner of the room.)

Don't be bashful, silly girl!
Don't be bashful, silly boy!
They won't eat you.
Show what you brought them.
(At last one shepherd boldly marches forward and lays his gifts before the Kings, then, bowing shyly, he retreats to his place.)

SHEPHERDS

Go on, go on, go on!
No! You go on!
Olives and quinces, apples and raisins,
nutmeg and myrtle, medlars and chestnuts,
this is all we shepherds can offer you.

KASPAR, MELCHIOR, BALTHAZAR

Thank you, thank you,
thank you kindly.
Thank you, thank you,
thank you kindly, too.
(A second shepherd crosses to the Kings, presents his gifts, and returns, bowing, to his place.)

SHEPHERDS

Citrons and lemons, musk and pomegranates,
goat-cheese and walnuts, figs and cucumbers,
this is all we shepherds can offer you.

KASPAR, MELCHIOR, BALTHAZAR

Thank you, thank you,
thank you kindly.
Thank you, thank you,
thank you kindly, too.

*(Taking courage from the others, a third shepherd presents
his gifts and returns to his place.)*

SHEPHERDS

Hazelnuts and camomile, mignonettes and laurel,
honeycombs and cinnamon, thyme, mint, and
            garlic,
this is all we shepherds can offer you.

KASPAR, MELCHIOR, BALTHAZAR

Thank you, thank you,
thank you kindly.
Thank you, thank you,
thank you kindly, too.

SHEPHERDS

Take them, eat them,
you are welcome.

(to the Page)

Take them, eat them,
you are welcome, too.

THE MOTHER

(beckoning to the young people)

Now won't you dance for them?

*(One young girl tries to flee. The young men pull her back,
and after much embarrassed nudging and pushing, she re-*

*turns. Meanwhile, Amahl fetches his shepherd's pipe and sits
at the fireplace beside an old bearded shepherd who already
holds his pipe. The two begin to play and the dance follows.)*

SHEPHERDS

Don't be bashful, silly girl!
Don't be bashful, silly boy!
They won't eat you!

*(The dance of the shepherds, which may include two or
more dancers, should combine the qualities of primitive folk
dancing and folk ritual. It is both an entertainment and a
ceremony of welcome and hospitality. The dancers are at
first shy and fearful at the realization that they are in the
presence of three great Kings, and their movements are at
times faltering and hesitant. But later, the dance assumes the
character of a tarantella, gaining in pace and sureness and
ending in a joyous frenzy.)*

(Balthazar rises to thank the dancers, then resumes his seat.)

BALTHAZAR

Thank you, good friends,
for your dances and your gifts.
But now we must bid you good night.
We have little time for sleep and a long journey
    ahead.

SHEPHERDS

Good night, my good Kings, good night and
    farewell.
The pale stars foretell that dawn is in sight.
Good night, my good Kings, good night and
    farewell.
The night wind foretells the day will be bright.

*(The shepherds pass before the Kings, bowing as they depart.
The Mother bids them good night at the door and for a
moment watches them down the road. After all have gone
their voices are still heard on the winter air.)*

ALL

Good night.
(Having closed the door, Amahl and the Mother bid the Kings good night. While the Mother prepares for herself a pallet of sheepskins on the floor, Amahl seizes his opportunity and speaks to King Kaspar.)

AMAHL

Excuse me, sir, amongst your magic stones
is there . . . is there one that could cure a crippled
    boy?

KASPAR

Eh?
(Defeated by Kaspar's deafness, Amahl goes sadly to his pallet of straw.)

AMAHL

Never mind . . . good night.

SHEPHERDS

(from off-stage)
Good night, good night.
The dawn is in sight.
Good night, farewell, good night.
(The Mother and Amahl have lain down on their pallets. The Kings, still sitting on the rude bench, settle themselves to sleep, leaning against each other. The Page curls himself up at their feet, his arms laid protectively over the rich gifts. His lantern has been placed on the floor by the fireplace, leaving only a dim glow in the room.)

(The lights in the hut are lowered completely to denote the passage of time. On the last chords of the interlude the interior of the hut is slowly lighted by the first pale rays of the dawn from the hills.)

THE MOTHER

(Still sitting on her pallet, the Mother cannot take her eyes from the treasure guarded by the Page.)

All that gold! All that gold!
I wonder if rich people know what to do with
    their gold!
Do they know how a child could be fed?
Do rich people know?
Do they know that a house can be kept warm all
    day with burning logs?
Do rich people know?
Do they know how to roast sweet corn on the fire?
Do they know?
Do they know how to fill a courtyard with doves?
Do they know?
Do they know how to milk a clover-fed goat?
Do they know how to spice hot wine on cold
    winter nights?
Do they know?
All that gold! All that gold!
Oh, what I could do for my child with that gold!
Why should it all go to a child they don't even
    know?
They are asleep. Do I dare?
If I take some they'll never miss it . . .

(Slowly she draws herself across the floor, dragging her body with her hands. Her words become a hushed whisper.)

For my child . . . for my child . . . for my child . . .

(As the Mother touches the gold, the Page is instantly aroused. He seizes her arm, crying to his masters. The Mother pulls frantically to free herself, dragging the Page into the center of the room. She still clutches the gold and jewels she has seized.)

The Page

Thief! Thief!

(The Kings awaken in confusion and rise.)

Melchior, Balthazar

What is it? What is it?

THE PAGE

I've seen her steal some of the gold.
She's a thief! Don't let her go!
She's stolen the gold!

KASPAR, MELCHIOR, BALTHAZAR

Shame! Shame!

THE PAGE

Give it back or I'll tear it out of you!

(Amahl awakens, at first completely bewildered. When he sees his mother in the hands of the Page, he helps himself up with his crutch and awkwardly hurls himself upon the Page, beating him hysterically and pulling his hair, in an effort to force the man to release the Mother.)

KINGS, THE PAGE

Give it back! Give it back!

AMAHL

Don't you dare!
Don't you dare, ugly man, hurt my mother!
I'll smash in your face!
I'll knock out your teeth!
Don't you dare!
Don't you dare, ugly man, hurt my mother!

(rushing to King Kaspar and tugging at his robe)

Oh, Mister King, don't let him hurt my mother!
My mother is good.
She cannot do anything wrong.
I'm the one who lies. I'm the one who steals.

(rushing back to attack the Page)

Don't you dare!
Don't you dare, ugly man, hurt my mother!
I'll break all your bones!
I'll bash in your head!

(At a sign from Kaspar, the Page releases the Mother. Still kneeling, she raises her arms toward her son. Choked by

tears, Amahl staggers toward her and, letting his crutch fall,
collapses, sobbing, into his mother's arms.)

MELCHIOR
Oh, woman, you may keep the gold.
The Child we seek doesn't need our gold.
On love, on love alone
He will build His kingdom.
His pierced hand will hold no scepter.
His haloed head will wear no crown.
His might will not be built on your toil.
Swifter than lightning
He will soon walk among us.
He will bring us new life and receive our death,
and the keys to His city belong to the poor.

(turning to the other Kings)

Let us leave, my friends.

(Freeing herself from Amahl's embrace, the Mother throws
herself on her knees before the Kings, spilling the gold she
has taken from her hands onto the carpet. Meanwhile, Amahl
is on his feet, leaning on his crutch.)

THE MOTHER
Oh, no, wait . . . take back your gold!
For such a King I've waited all my life.
And if I weren't so poor
I would send a gift of my own to such a child.

AMAHL
But, Mother, let me send him my crutch.
Who knows, he may need one,
and this I made myself.

THE MOTHER
But that you can't, you can't!

(The Mother moves to stop him as he starts to raise the
crutch. Amahl lifts the crutch. There is a complete hush in
the room. The boy takes one step toward the Kings, then
realizes that he has moved without the help of his crutch.)

AMAHL

(in a whisper)
    I walk, Mother . . .
    I walk, Mother!

KASPAR

He walks . . .

MELCHIOR

He walks . . .

BALTHAZAR

He walks . . .

THE MOTHER

He walks . . .
(Step by step, Amahl very slowly makes his way toward the Kings, the crutch held before him in his outstretched hands. The Mother rises and draws back, almost fearful of the miracle she beholds.)

KASPAR, MELCHIOR, BALTHAZAR

It is a sign from the Holy Child.
We must give praise to the new-born King.
We must praise Him.
This is a sign from God!
(Having placed the crutch in the outstretched hands of King Kaspar, Amahl moves uncertainly to the center of the room.)

(With growing confidence, Amahl begins to jump and caper about the room.)

AMAHL

Look, Mother, I can dance,
I can jump, I can run!

KASPAR, MELCHIOR, BALTHAZAR

Truly, he can dance,
he can jump, he can run!
(The Mother and the Kings follow Amahl breathlessly, fearing that he may fall. At last, as he turns a clumsy pirouette, Amahl does stumble and fall to the floor.)

THE MOTHER
(She goes quickly to Amahl and lifts him from the floor.)
Please, my darling, be careful now.
You must take care not to hurt yourself.

KASPAR, MELCHIOR, BALTHAZAR
Oh, good woman, you must not be afraid.
For he is loved by the Son of God.

KASPAR
Oh, blessed child, may I touch you?

MELCHIOR
Oh, blessed child, may I touch you?

BALTHAZAR
Oh, blessed child, may I touch you?
(One at a time, the Kings pass before Amahl and lay their hands upon him. Then each goes across to take up his gift to the Child, ready to begin the departure. The Page comes last, prostrating himself on the floor before Amahl.)

THE PAGE
Oh, blessed child, may I touch you?

AMAHL
(enjoying a first taste of self-importance)
Well, I don't know if I'm going to let *you* touch
me.

THE MOTHER
(in gentle reproof)
Amahl!

AMAHL
Oh, all right . . . but just once.
Look, Mother, I can fight,
I can work, I can play!
Oh, Mother, let me go with the Kings!
I want to take the crutch to the Child myself.

KASPAR, MELCHIOR, BALTHAZAR
Yes, good woman, let him come with us!
We'll take good care of him,
we'll bring him back on a camel's back.
(Amahl and his mother are together apart from the others, she kneeling before him.)

THE MOTHER
Do you really want to go?

AMAHL
Yes, Mother.
THE MOTHER
Are you sure, sure, sure?

AMAHL
I'm sure!
THE MOTHER
Yes, I think you should go,
and bring thanks to the Child yourself.

AMAHL
(not quite believing his ears)
Are you sure, sure, sure?

THE MOTHER
Go on, get ready.

KASPAR
What did she say?

BALTHAZAR
She said he can come.

KASPAR
Oh, lovely, lovely, lo . . .
(Again Balthazar restrains Kaspar's exuberance.)

BALTHAZAR
Kaspar!

THE MOTHER
What to do with your crutch?

AMAHL
You can tie it to my back.

THE MOTHER
Don't forget to wear your hat!

AMAHL
I shall always wear my hat.

THE MOTHER
So, my darling, good-bye!

AMAHL, MOTHER
So, my darling, good-bye!
I shall miss you very much.

THE MOTHER
Wash your ears!

AMAHL
Yes, I promise.

THE MOTHER
Don't tell lies!

AMAHL

No, I promise.
Feed my bird!

THE MOTHER

Yes, I promise.

AMAHL

Watch the cat!

THE MOTHER

Yes, I promise.

AMAHL

I shall miss you very much.

SHEPHERDS

(from off-stage)
Shepherds, arise!

MELCHIOR

Are you ready?

AMAHL

Yes, I'm ready.

MELCHIOR

Let's go then.
(Led by the Page, who has taken up his burdens and the
heavy lamp, the Three Kings start their stately procession
out of the cottage.)

SHEPHERDS

Come, oh shepherds, come outside.
All the stars have left the sky.
Oh, sweet dawn, oh, dawn of peace.

(Amahl rushes into his mother's arms, bidding her goodbye, then hurries to catch up with the departing Kings. Having taken his place at the end of the procession, Amahl begins to play his pipes as he goes. Outside, the soft colors of dawn are brightening the sky, and a few great flakes of snow have begun to fall upon the road.)

(The Mother stands alone in the doorway of the cottage. Then she goes outside to wave once more to Amahl, as he turns to her, just before he disappears at the bend in the road.)

(The curtain falls very slowly.)

The End